Lifestyles of Southern California

Personal Sanctuaries by KAA Design Group

Lifestyles of Southern California

Personal Sanctuaries by KAA Design Group

They turned the country

up on its side,

and everything loose

fell into California.

Frank Lloyd Wright[*]

As one went to Europe

to see the living past,

so one must visit Southern California

to observe the future.

Alison Lurie

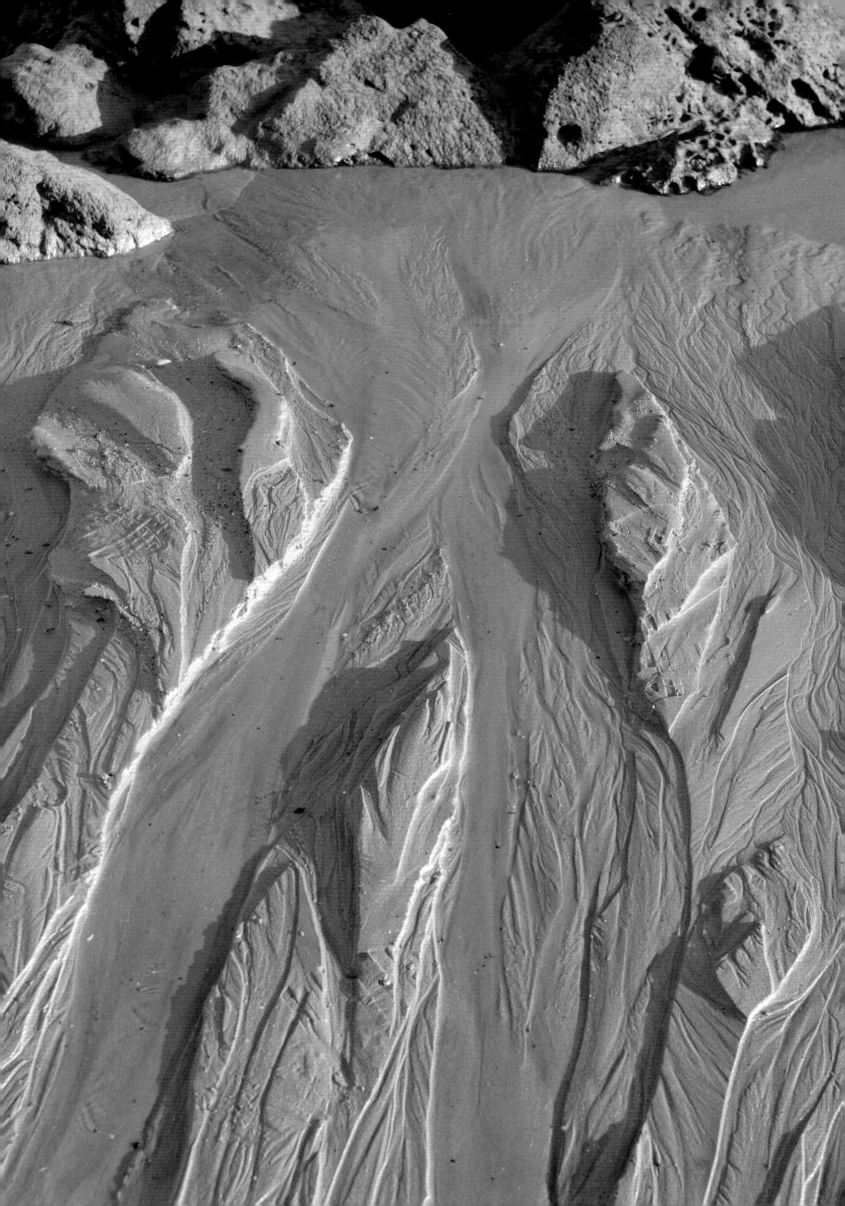

Southern California — home to one of the most geographically, ethnically, and culturally diverse areas in the world — is rife with contradictions. In a place where one can snow ski and surf in the same day, people from around the globe live side by side, and the cuisine of every country on the planet is readily available. The unremarkable, casually dressed person you see walking down the street could be a wealthy entertainer or a self-made billionaire.

From the 19th century — a period when Americans were encouraged to "go west"— to the contemporary moment, Southern California and its image have been inextricably linked and mutually reinforcing. A particular breed of open-minded individual with an adventurous spirit continues to be drawn to the region, which is a natural attractor for creative people who thrive in an environment free from traditional limits or boundaries. There is an inherent, palpable optimism in the spirit of those who have risked the safety and security of more conventional lives and migrated here to the edge: not only the physical edge of the country, but also the edge of imagination. The gold miners of the mid-1800s, the aspiring stars who come to Hollywood every year seduced by images of California propagated by the film industry, the engineers, writers, and Silicon Valley entrepreneurs all share a common vision: the dream of riches both material and spiritual — and a better way of life. Lured by the temperate climate, possibilities of prosperity, the prospect of starting life over with a clean slate, and a healthy outdoor lifestyle, these modern-day pioneers are richly rewarded for having taken the chance. Though they may not realize their dreams precisely as imagined, they have each succeeded in what is, for most of us, the far more difficult task of shedding the torpor of everyday life and its constraints to gamble on the unknown, accepting the possibility that the outcome may differ from their expectations.

From the 19th century – a period when Americans were encouraged to "go west" – to the contemporary moment, Southern California and its image have been inextricably linked and mutually reinforcing.

The stories in this volume feature individuals and families who have taken this journey and succeeded. Having attained success in their various professions, they then turned their focus to their personal realms. Through the process of building their private sanctuaries, they all surpassed their previous notions of the function of a residence to create homes that more accurately express and reflect who they are and how they want to live. Their homes facilitate interaction with one another, with their communities, and with the land in ways that complement and ameliorate their personal and professional lives. Designing their own homes is the logical extension of their decisions to live in Southern California, one that continues to have an equally dramatic impact on their lives. It is the ultimate expression of the desire to live precisely as one chooses.

The following residences set the stage for lifestyles that demonstrate personal versions of the California Dream. The opposite of a dream is reality. In essence, the unique California lifestyle represents a fantastic hybrid of these two seemingly opposing states. In this book, the reality is the manifestation of the dream in built form: personal sanctuaries. These distinctive homes translate the best elements of the California Dream into authentic, genuine constructions of reality. Dream on...

Lifestyles of Southern California
Personal Sanctuaries by KAA Design Group

Although many of us daydream about turning our lives upside down and making an enormous leap across cultural and physical landscapes, in reality acting on those fantasies is for the courageous few. Those adventurous enough are rewarded countless times over for taking the risk, often in ways they would never have been able to anticipate.

When they dreamed of having a beach home in Southern California and chose to uproot and transplant their family from England to the western edge of North America, the owners put into motion a thrilling, life-altering experience. Their relocation is a study in contrasts: from urban density to a densely suburban environment, from a primarily damp climate to one of the most mild where outdoor living is possible year-round, and from a relatively conservative society to a culture that attracts like-minded people seeking a more relaxed, creative lifestyle.

Imagine the radical shift in outlook that results from a family leaving a London terrace house with an interior focus and moving halfway across the world with the opportunity to create their own courtyard house on the beach that literally expands horizons by promoting connections to the outside world, and the Pacific Ocean. From London's Portland Place, a heavily trafficked street, to Hermosa Beach's Strand, a pedestrian street with lively outdoor activity, the move was from a discreetly enclosed district to a place of limitless possibilities.

Those adventurous enough are rewarded countless times over for taking the risk, often in ways they would never have been able to anticipate.

Living Life on the Edge

In much the same way that travel to foreign countries alters the perception of one's own home, moving to such a dramatically different environment encourages viewing the world through fresh eyes. To facilitate that new perception, a key element of the design is transparency — literal and metaphorical. Visitors are treated to a stunning ocean view through a series of layered openings leading from the entrance to the beach. A horizontal slot of glass separating the first and second stories focuses on the border of ocean and sky; a line of light that penetrates the entire interior. The second story floats above this horizon line, lifting the dwelling into the loftier spaces of the sky and the imagination. This design highlights the meeting between sea and sky and also fosters transformation in the lives of clients in the process of discovering new personal horizons.

The design of the home reflects the family's appreciation for looking beyond the safe and traditional to arrive at the best solution, even if that involves a degree of risk-taking. Deep cantilevers and long spans represent a structural bravado, ultimately receding into minimal volumes that form a background to the site and frame the activities of daily life. Clear, open space on the lower floor flows outward to the horizon. The home wraps itself from the front to the back of the site, creating a roofless garden courtyard that takes advantage of the temperate climate. The formal geometry of interlocking rectangles wheels around this courtyard, which creates the core around which the house turns. Most spaces in the house, including the master bedroom, communicate with this central open space, which pulls down a shaft of sky into the center of the house. Visible from anywhere in the house, the courtyard is a safe, controlled nucleus for small children to play. One of the joys of living in Southern California is the ability to spend time comfortably outdoors year-round.

Several contrary elements enliven the home's design. The first floor flows as a single open space while the second floor hovers as a horizontal bar of discrete rooms. The ground level wraps itself around the courtyard and is open from east to west; the top level is composed of less open spaces that provide a sense of enclosure. The comforts of a more traditional home are embedded in the private rooms of the top floor where fireplaces, tongue and groove mahogany wood, and office nooks are scaled to recall snug English houses.

The limestone wall at the main entry protects the house from the busy street, grounding it in memory and history at the same time as it negotiates the transition from earth to air. A 'wood tower' punctuates all levels, connecting the ground with the sky, containing the special area of a window seat on the main living floor and an office on the second floor. Through its vertical orientation, the tower serves as counterpoint to the ocean's horizontal line, adding complexity and formal richness to the overall massing. The tower, the views to the ocean, and the rectangles that turn ninety degrees to each other at three edges of the site form façades that face westward to the ocean, northward to the mountains, and vertically to the sky.

Following in the footsteps of numerous other innovative thinkers attracted to this area known as a nexus of creative freedom, and renewal of the mind and body, the family has discovered that the lifestyle offered here is as re-energizing, inspiring, and stimulating as they had hoped. This home is the physical manifestation of the clients' spiritual journey from England to California, a blend of old and the new, familiar and comfortable, avant-garde and minimalist.

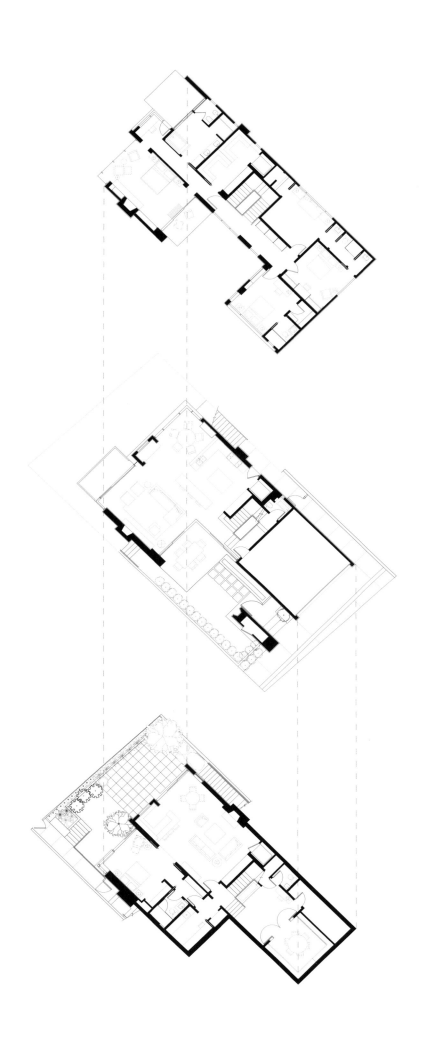

The limestone wall at the
main entry protects the house
from the busy street, grounding it
in memory and history while
simultaneously negotiating the
transition from earth to air.

Deep cantilevers and long spans, representing a structural bravado, ultimately recede into minimal volumes that form a background to the site and frame the activities of daily life.

At some point, we are all seduced by feelings of wanderlust — a passion to explore distant lands, discover different cultures, and view the world through the eyes of another. One of the greatest benefits of travel becomes evident only when we return to our own homes with an enhanced capacity to experience our environments and our lives anew.

This young family's home in the Pacific Palisades, with its outdoor lifestyle and respect for nature, incorporates numerous references to their enthusiasm for Asia and the South Sea Islands. A cluster of interlocking pavilions surrounds a large, two-story atrium forming the literal and metaphorical center of the home. From there to the property's edge, nature enters and retreats as gently and as constantly as the tide ebbs and flows.

Cultivating close connections is a vital, recurring theme in this home: connections to family, to nature, and to aesthetics. The atrium, while formally beautiful, also plays a critical role in the family's daily life. The father was adamant in his desire to see his children playing from any room in the home—the placement of the atrium at the core and the large wood-framed windows make that possible. This central atrium connects to a dining room and generous living areas on the first floor, functioning as a semi-public realm where the family gathers and entertains. Surrounded by other rooms and lit by clerestory windows, it almost feels like an exterior courtyard that, over time, had been covered by a roof. The open walkway on the upper level acts as a transition, a sandwiched layer of space between the atrium and more private spaces of the home.

Nature is everywhere. This was made possible, in part, by limiting the footprint of the house, allowing the landscape to occupy a large percentage of the site. There is a constant give and take between solid and void, nature and building, inside and outside. When a sliding wall opens, the pond enters the interior visually and acoustically. Corner windows come together without frames, further dissolving barriers between interior and exterior. Gardens at the edges of rooms draw the eye outward, and reflected light from the gardens bounces off exposed wood ceilings and into the interior, creating a subtle, green hue softening the home's harder edges.

...nature enters and retreats as gently and as constantly
as the tide ebbs and flows.

Each of the park-like setting's four gardens represents a unique travel experience in Indonesia, setting the stage for a seamless combination of indoor and outdoor spaces, bridging design and nature. The gardens meet the house in a series of roofless rooms, and, like Russian dolls, create special places nested within other spaces. These havens of meditation and leisure also reflect four different psychic conditions.

The Zen Garden takes its inspiration from the late 15th-century Ryoan-ji rock garden in Kyoto, Japan. Five elements represent the five Confucian virtues of meditation: politeness is embodied in a flat stone bridge, benevolence is expressed by a shallow bowl that holds water, wisdom is reflected in a wonderfully gnarled old rock, fidelity is represented by a juniper, and justice is symbolized by a boulder balanced on a narrow point.

The Great Lawn is an enclosed space surrounded by a lush tropical garden. Curvilinear stone walls hold back dense topical plantings. One can easily imagine a tiger pouncing out of the jungle-like landscape. The grassy enclosure references the English colonial tradition of imported lawns, a memory of moister climates and more expansive landscapes. It acknowledges the transplantation of California's multicultural population while it invites the association with classical literature that characterizes the great south lawn at the garden of Stowe in England.

The enclosed Jewel Box Garden almost penetrates the formal dining room. Light bouncing off stone surfaces, reminiscent of Japanese contemplative gardens, sparkles and shimmers during the day. At night, illuminated candles shine from stone outcroppings.

The Water Garden — a place of re-centering and rejuvenation — contains a Koi pond, bridges, waterfalls, and a Southeast Asian lanai that traditionally serves as a place of gathering and community. With its steeply pitched roof resting on sturdy columns, the lanai is large enough to shelter an exterior dining and sitting room. A large glowing lantern hangs in the middle, a relic of a movie set that ties the family's personal history to the garden's memory. When the home's walls are open, the water garden becomes a large outdoor room, allowing the family's social life to flow outward, capturing the entire landscape within the domestic sphere.

The home facilitates family connections and a powerful relationship to nature, but also has ties to the aesthetics and architectural history of California. The creation of areas that allow everyone to be together, yet at the same time, permit everyone to have privacy, has an architectural precedent in Rudolf Schindler's Kings Road House (1922) in West Hollywood — a combination studio and home he designed for himself, his wife, and another couple. Each person was allocated an interior and exterior room, while several indoor and outdoor living spaces provided opportunities for them to gather collectively. This home and Schindler's share a similar natural color palette and modernist treatment of windows with large expanses of glass overlooking and giving access to gardens.

As Schindler viewed Southern California through the eyes of a European transplanted halfway across the world to this foreign landscape, this family has incorporated the fruits of their own wanderlust into their home, their family, and their lifestyle. Insights gained from travel, exposure to other modes of living, and excitement of witnessing places and customs foreign to them, all contributed to the home's ultimate design.

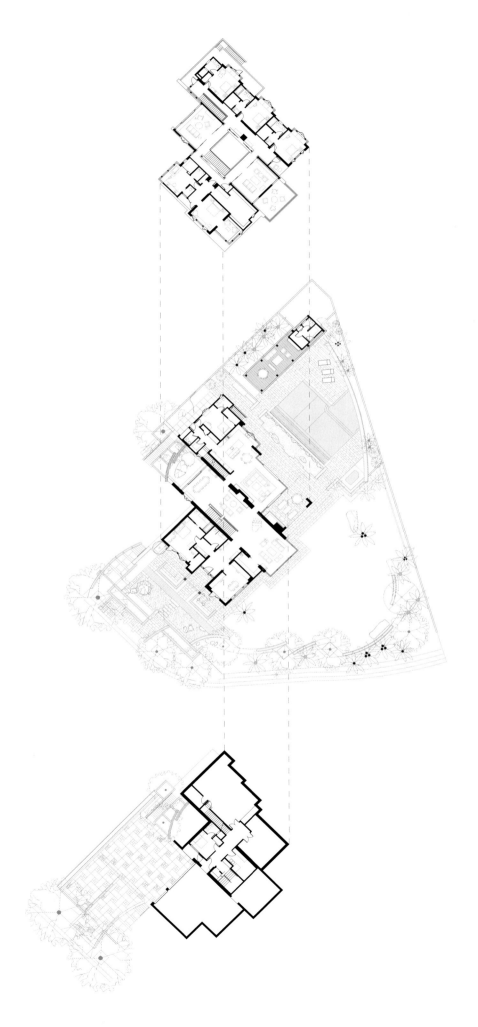

A cluster of
interlocking pavilions
surrounds the large,
two-story atrium that is the
literal and metaphorical
center of the home.

For many of us, some of our happiest childhood memories are of the hours we spent snuggled in our beds being read to by a parent. Of these fantastic tales of exotic, far-away places, the stories that resonate the most are those whose details render a clear mental picture of the setting, characters, and events, allowing the audience to fully engage in the action.

Scheherazade's *One Thousand and One Nights* — with its portrayals of romance and adventure set in meticulously detailed spaces and buildings, surrounded by veils of mystery and glittering with lush surfaces — immediately came to mind when our clients first discovered this property — half of the legendary estate, Mi Sueño (My Dream), designed by Bertram Goodhue in 1917. They were intrigued by the home's rich history and by the challenge of bringing it back to life.

The decaying home had previously been much larger, having at one point been bisected to yield two separate residences. Even in abandonment, Mi Sueño had enough traces of its original grandeur to warrant a significant renovation. It was an important part of California's architectural history with its romantic intermingling of Spanish Baroque and Moroccan exoticism reinterpreted by one of this area's greatest architects. Our intervention has resulted in a home with thick stucco walls, beautifully proportioned rooms, axial planning connecting the residence to gardens, and a stunning ornamental program. The interior design required the same level of research and attention to detail as the architectural renovation and addition.

The restoration focused on two main spaces: the foyer, originally a vestibule leading to the formal dining room, and the dining room itself, restored to its original elegant state as the new living room. The rest of the home, including servants' quarters, was reconceived to replicate the details of the original. The promise of saving two grand rooms and removing a rabbit warren of spaces that distorted their former character created a story so lasting, compelling, and persuasive that it captivated its owners as Scheherazade did her audience.

...portrayals of romance and adventure set in meticulously detailed spaces and buildings, surrounded by veils of mystery and glittering with lush surfaces...

Exploring like an amateur archaeologist, the client's curiosity was rewarded and his excitement increased when he discovered remnants that provided clues and inspired a vision of what could be. Buried fragments and artifacts surfaced from the excavated earth and were displayed in the basement for evaluation. These historical elements were carefully restored and duplicated, and are encountered throughout the home and grounds: in paving, ceiling details, furniture, and tiles.

The Moorish theme is pervasive. The bathroom, an entirely new creation, is faithful to Goodhue's fanciful and ornate conceptions, and appears to be space original to the home. Covered in cobalt blue and traditional Moroccan, star-patterned tiles, the bathroom's generous spaces invoke the harem of Topkapi Palace, distinguished for its brilliant red, blue, and green Iznik tile and its luxurious, internally-focused spaces meant for coddling the sultan's wives. More a formal bathing complex than a simple room, the bathroom's vaulted side corridors access deep-set showers.

Delicate wooden lattices found in traditional Islamic homes appear in cabinets, in screens separating rooms, in shutters, and in the master bathroom. The intricate wooden canopy over the bathtub references the rich wooden walls and canopied enclosures of Islamic palaces. The screens diffuse light into speckled patterns, allowing partial views from one space to another. The home is revealed through a series of "veils" complemented by gossamer curtains. The boudoir is a fantastical space of mirrors, latticework, and spaces that might store Scheherazade's jeweled costumes. Lighting fixtures with colored and prismatic glass inserts reflect the fragments of colored stained glass in the original windows above the front entrance and at the landing of the rear stair. These rooms are designed to honor rituals of bathing and celebrating the human body.

Expanding upon the fictional narrative of a home rebuilt with a patina of age and a texture of memory, the decoration is purposefully eclectic. Historical reconstructions of antique furniture and custom-designed pieces blend with contemporary furnishings and modern appliances. A new sofa sits on an antique Persian rug, the custom-designed entry table is ornamented with a carved fish, bedposts are inspired by Moroccan precedents, and custom hand-dyed curtains from India are bordered with decorative appliqués.

The Moorish fantasies at the heart of Goodhue's design are also evident in the home's dreamlike gardens, elements that recall the pleasure gardens of Moorish palaces. The north courtyard replaced an existing pedestrian service court, creating a new landscape focus for the home. The 1950s pool is surrounded by whimsical white statues of eagles that look modern, but were retained as part of the home's historical narrative. A new spa reinstates Goodhue's Moorish theme, recalling water features such as those found in the Court of the Myrtles in the Alhambra.

The garden spaces, fountains, and swimming pool celebrate nature and water's rejuvenating essence. A courtyard next to the dining room looks south to the 1917 long pool and cascade. Beautiful new tile mosaics restore those areas to their former splendor. The new front entrance includes a pool shaped as a Moorish star with a flowing water channel similar to the secluded courtyards of the Alhambra with their murmuring rustle of water, cooling in the hot summers of southern Spain. These water features, originating in historical precedents, extend Mi Sueño's vision by fusing memory and meditation.

The dream of an enchanting home, embodied in the home's name and still visible in fragments throughout the property, inspired our seamless reweaving of old and new. Mi Sueño, reborn as a single residence, is a museum-quality sanctuary: at once livable, down to earth, and graceful. As in Scheherazade's chronicle, this couple set out on a multi-year journey, a magic carpet ride, to realize their dream of creating their own Moorish-inspired oasis.

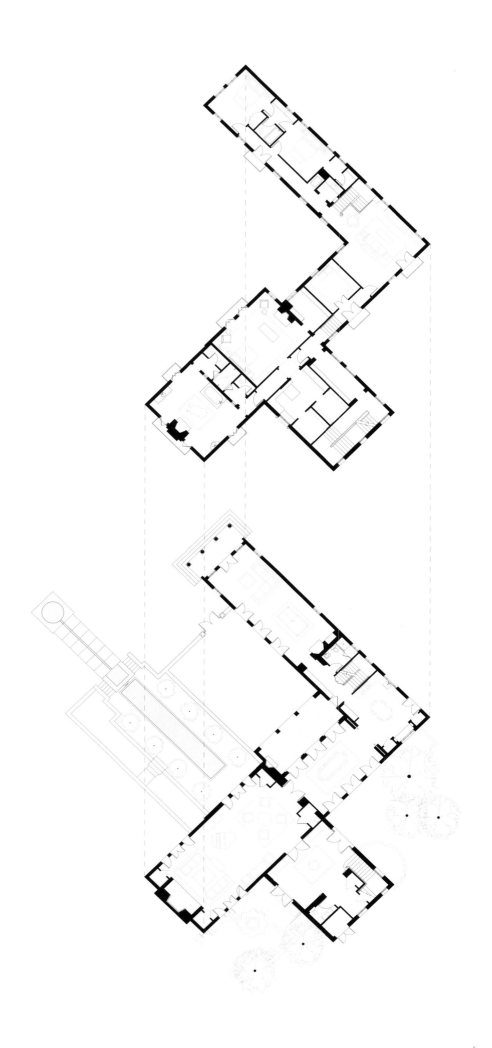

The Moorish fantasies at the heart of Goodhue's design are also evident in the home's dreamlike gardens, elements that recall the pleasure gardens of Moorish palaces.

Like thousands of others before them, this family was drawn to the coast by the promise of enjoying time outdoors in every season and by the relaxed pace and healthy lifestyle. The expansive view of the glittering Pacific Ocean, the warm, relaxing breezes, and the clear California light have always been reasons enough to long to live in a beach home, but there is also historical evidence to show that living in a well-designed environment can support and even enhance one's physical, emotional, and spiritual life.

This beach home for a family with young children represents the next stage in the evolution of California Modernism; an homage both to Schindler and to the principles related to physical and mental well-being that are embodied in great Modernist architecture. Located just one half block from the beach in a high-density, residential neighborhood, the home's outdoor spaces are raised off the ground and the third floor living spaces merge to create one large, comfortable room. The inverted living pattern liberates the family from the earthly world by placing the more public areas on the uppermost floor. Here, dramatic natural light and architectural space play off spectacular ocean views framed by floor-to-ceiling, transparent, moveable walls. The partially submerged beach room invites the outside in by providing ample exterior space for the family to relax underneath the house.

The design employs a unique spatial language that addresses tight site constraints and the cheerful urban clutter of Southern California beach town walk streets. Restrictions such as zoning laws dictated a design response that brought together sun angles, views, slope, and allowable square footages into a comprehensive floor plan. The home is oriented on its long side from north to south, with a west-facing façade overlooking the Pacific Ocean and an east façade looking backward to neighbors as close at six feet away. The resulting language of form owes its depth and clarity to its roots in California Modernism, a tradition with formal, material, bodily, and spiritual goals.

The legacy of Modernism saturates this house with echoes of a transformative way of living.

To maximize the potential of the site, the eastern façade's plaster walls are more solid and private, but the northern, southern, and western facades are completely open, capturing views stretching from the Palos Verdes Peninsula to Catalina Island and Malibu. Three-dimensional interlocking volumes implode around a central stair leading to the top floor where space and light conversely explode into a series of interconnected spaces. An interior courtyard and two generous balconies at this level bring the front yard up to the sky and provide ample space to barbecue, dine, and lounge outdoors. Opaque interior walls perpendicular to the views form expansive surfaces upon which to display an extensive collection of Modern art.

The exterior of the home provides an explicit map of the site. While the eastern façade's nearly solid white plaster wall gives the family privacy, the open, western façade reveals extensive floor to ceiling glass. The southern façade splits down the middle: the east half is a plaster wall penetrated by rectangular windows covered with awnings, and the west side is glass walls and protruding balconies. The deep balconies and awnings protect the artwork from the damaging effects of the sun. The main entrance faces onto the walk street, offering a generous spatial sequence from the front gate to the front door. The second floor cantilevers from this corner and floats above the entry, creating a cubic volume of space below and making the entrance a ceremonial device as well as a much-welcomed street presence.

The legacy of Modernism saturates this house with echoes of a transformative way of living. By referencing local traditions such as those that Schindler developed and adapting them to the specifics of the site and the needs of the family, this home establishes a proposal for the design of homes in the beach towns of Southern California. It elevates its surroundings by example and its inhabitants with its dramatic views, uplifted spaces, and sense of spare, yet sumptuous well-being. With its generous spaces and permeability to the out-of-doors, the home maintains the utopian belief that a well designed environment can support and enhance one's physical, emotional, and spiritual life.

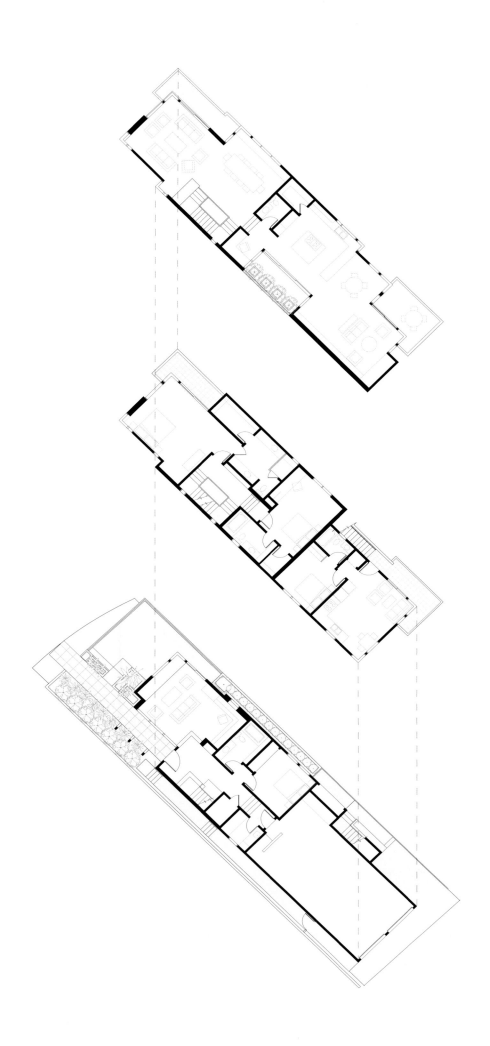

An adventurous family with young children and a passion for exploring remote, far-flung corners of the world travels not just for the excitement of experiencing exotic environments, but also as a respite from chaotic daily life. Exposure to diverse cultures gives them a deep appreciation for the rich woods, colorful fabrics, tropical palettes, and elegant simplicity of Asian craftsmanship. While influenced by numerous modes of living throughout the world, this family was most inspired by the possibility of infusing the tranquil, Balinese lifestyle into their home and lives.

In Bali, known as "the island of artists," artistic expression touches all aspects of life; it is a gift shared by everyone. The pursuit of art as a vital part of Balinese culture struck a personal chord with this family whose home is located in a similarly temperate climate near the sea. This three-story, inverted floor plan reflects the Balinese preference for vertical living with a panoramic view of the landscape. The home evokes images of tropical climates and outdoor lifestyles, where physical transitions between architecture and nature all but dissolve beneath a broad canopy of a sheltering wooden ceiling.

To take best advantage of the spectacular coastline views from this urban beach site, the more public living spaces are located on the top floor and the more private spaces on the entry level. This upper floor is where everything happens — it is the hub of family activity and the place permeated by nature. Exposed wood roof beams and ceilings float above an open floor plan that contains the main living spaces of the great room, the kitchen, the dining area, and the outdoor room.

In Bali, known as "the island of artists,"
artistic expression touches all aspects of life;
it is a gift shared by everyone.

Low partition walls create visually discrete areas while simultaneously preserving the appearance of a single volume that spans the entire floor, opening outward to the light, air, and view of the South Bay landscape. An operable wall at one end of this floor can fully open up to the outside room, seamlessly extending the public space to the exterior. This exterior room has ocean views, an outdoor spa, built-in barbeque, and a second kitchen for outdoor entertaining. Fireplaces at opposite ends of the home anchor it to its site and create spaces where — depending on the weather — it is possible to spend time inside, outside, or both, beside the comfort of a glowing fire.

The lower floors — solid masses of stone and plaster — have a more private interior focus, but even in the most personal spaces like the master bedroom, the boundary between interior and exterior is softened by an ocean view terrace. The informal "beach room" at the lowest level extends out to a patio at the south corner that ties the residence back to its street community, breaking the monolithic volume typical of many urban beach communities. The rooms collected under the hovering roof reflect the inspiration and form of Balinese architecture. The large pavilion on the top floor, the site of the main living spaces, hovers above the world of the street below. The two fireplaces — one inside and one outside — form a spiritual compass connecting fire, air, sea, and mountains. In accepting cool breezes and framing distant views, the home presents an invitation to a voyage in which the inhabitants can imagine a serene life on their very own private island.

The home offers a variety of experiences: exterior open spaces reminiscent of the generous verandas of the Balinese traditional house, lattice walls of the Great Room, filmy curtained seclusion in the private spaces, and romantic places of repose. Filtered light, views of the sea, warm and rich interiors, and expansive sitting areas suggest a carefree life of leisure.

In addition to the Balinese references, artifacts accumulated over a lifetime of journeys are displayed throughout the home: a rain drum, Nigerian weaving sticks, Kuba cloth from Zaire, a Tibetan ceremonial costume, and an African side table. These souvenirs provoke memories of the various adventures the family has undertaken together and also serve as constant reminders of the value of being receptive to the gifts other places and lifestyles have to offer. This home is a place for family members and their guests to relax and lose themselves; a chance to embrace nature and make living an art, and art an integral part of living.

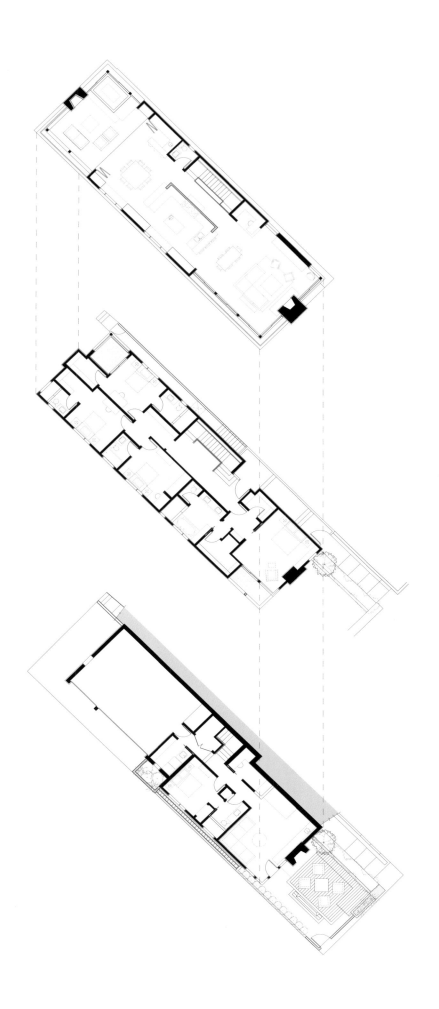

217

…a chance to embrace nature and make living an art, and art an integral part of living.

Wouldn't it be nice if, as you grow older, you could continue to live in the same beach community you've come to love and feel a part of, but in a wonderful new home ideally suited to your changing needs? Imagine how great it would be to downsize — to reduce scale without reducing quality; to enhance, not compromise, your lifestyle.

For this couple of "empty nesters," the perfect home is now one that requires minimal maintenance: simple yet elegant, clean and modern, and centrally located with a panoramic view. They began by choosing a smaller property in their long-term neighborhood so they could remain part of the vital, active, local life they had enjoyed for years and maintain their cherished connection to the ocean.

Inspiration was close at hand, in fact literally in their own back yard. The local lifeguard station, popularized through the music of groups such as The Beach Boys (who actually grew up in this neighborhood), has become a symbol of the Southern California lifestyle. From the elevated vantage point of the station, the lifeguard has sweeping views of the beach and ocean and is able to look after the immediate community. In a similar way, this compact, 2,000-square-foot residence with its clearly articulated volumes, takes advantage of its position on a corner to engage the neighborhood in much the same way as a lifeguard station engages the beach.

Parallels to lifeguard stations go beyond the merely iconic. This home can be closed up at a moment's notice, similar to shuttering a lifeguard station at the end of the day, allowing the family to travel and come and go with ease.

A floating wooden box crowned by a butterfly roof shelters the ground floor living space. This level hovers above the main space, allowing the family to keep watch over both the immediate neighborhood and the ocean beyond. Clerestory windows cap the seven-foot high exterior walls, providing natural light and ventilation and maintaining the enclosure necessary to screen the more intimate activities of bedrooms and bathroom housed on this level. In these spaces, structural steel columns are pulled inward, away from the exterior walls, and are expressed as freestanding elements that highlight functional differences between enclosure and frame. Wall panels are expressed as thin planes set into metal joints. Metal is also used in a horizontal band along the roof, which catches the sun. Rather than channel rainwater through a typical downspout, this function has been transformed into a piece of natural theater by employing a rain chain, a series of metal cups that drip water into each other and dangle in the wind. Exposed concrete walls and welded steel frames are built with exacting precision. In keeping with the desire for low maintenance, these details are the home's only ornamentation.

Daily life occurs primarily within one shared room without interior partitions — a transparent pavilion on the main level that contains a combination kitchen, dining, and living space. This more public part of the home is constructed using a modern palette of concrete, steel, and glass. To increase the sense of spaciousness, the glass walls open to make the exterior terraces and surrounding gardens part of the interior living spaces. With the doors open, the first floor is transformed into an outdoor space. The wood siding that skins the second floor façade wraps on the underside as a ceiling, intensifying the sense of being in the open space below a lifeguard tower.

To preserve precious ground area that the residents wanted to leave open to facilitate contact with the lively neighborhood street life, a tandem carport substitutes for an enclosed garage. The bottom floor pulls back from the minimum setback lines to create four exterior rooms — an outdoor dining terrace, a garden, a sitting area, and the tandem carport.

On the edge of this primarily transparent base, the functions that require opacity — the powder room, kitchen, entertainment center, and stair — are positioned next to solid concrete walls that anchor the building to its site, creating a rhythm of solid and void on the façade. At this level, glass walls allow light and air to enter, while on the second floor more traditional "punched" window openings pierce the paneled enclosure. To control this high level of transparency on a street with significant pedestrian activity and in a house on display, pocket shading systems may be raised or lowered electronically, and landscaping further buffers the house from the street.

This small home carries the weight of history and reference in its light frame. Despite its height and prominent siting, the scale relates it to the neighboring beach bungalows, a comparison made all the more explicit by the choice of exposed wood siding on the exterior of the second floor. The design's limited kit of parts refers equally to the great California tradition of ranch houses and the warm Modern designs of significant local architects such as Cliff May or Charles and Ray Eames. But the house also recalls the Modernism of the International Style through the formal allusions of its open plan and the extensive use of exposed materials left in their pure state.

Parallels to lifeguard stations go beyond the merely iconic. This home can be closed up at a moment's notice, similar to shuttering a lifeguard station at the end of the day, allowing the family to travel and to come and go with ease. Like the flying roof form that shelters the lifeguard from the intensity of the midday sun, the butterfly roof gives this home a kinetic quality, acknowledging its multiple exposures as it sits in the center of the neighborhood. Neighbors have remarked that this is the house that keeps guard on the street, bringing people together and providing a sense of grounding. Like the lifeguard station that inspired it, it stands out; the home is a landmark, and it soars.

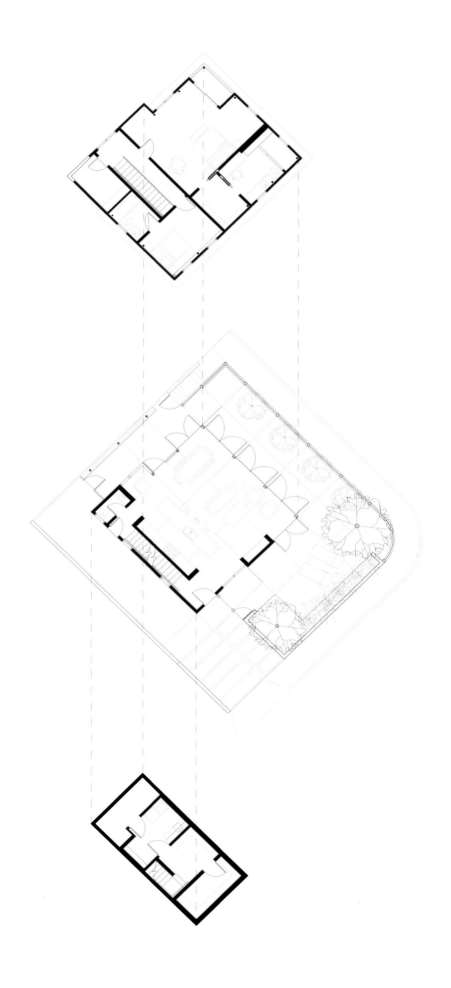

The house recalls the Modernism
of the International Style through
the formal allusions of its
open plan and the extensive
use of exposed materials
left in their pure state.

What if you could actually live in the tree house of your childhood dreams but on a grander scale and a variety of spaces, both indoors and out? You would have your own private sanctuary, protected by nature and shared with the people closest to you. In theory, that's exactly what this young family of five does. From the instant ground was broken for construction, their home became a center of interest for the neighbors. On daily visits to the site, some hopped the fence to get a closer look, others became acquainted with people they had lived next door to for thirty years but had not previously met.

The tree-lined street in the "tree section" of a beach community has a spectacular vantage point from the top of its hill and is a culturally, historically, and architecturally diverse area. The community in transition has a blend of lots built to their maximum allowable square footage and smaller homes that have weathered the test of time through the care and devotion of their owners. The challenge was to respond to the diversity while simultaneously creating a design that would draw from the eclecticism.

Inspiration came from two of California's more important architectural traditions — European Modernism adapted to suit Southern California's cultural climate and Mediterranean influences dating back at least to the beginnings of the rancho lands underlying this area's beach communities. The home speaks with a Southern California accent with traces of both Rudolf Schindler's own tilt-up concrete residence/studio in West Hollywood and Wallace Neff's interpretations of Mediterranean villas.

Clean lines, impeccable details, and exquisite materials elegantly bind the architecture of the Classical past to the Modernist future, demonstrating that Modernism can be as timeless as Classicism. The corner window — an index of the Modernist themes of truth in materials and blurring boundaries — meets the thick plaster walls, punched windows, extended cornices, and high towers emblematic of Mediterranean architecture; a blending of forms characteristic of the work of many architects building in this region. Where this home differs

The childhood dream of a tree house is a club you control the access to, but also share. This home with its tree house references is the neighborhood club that this family dreamt of — one that stitches together the diversity of the immediate neighborhood and the broader regional context.

is in its references to the immediate context and to the larger vocabulary of Southern California architecture, and in the precise, evocative, detailed material expression of the design. These differences are visible from the largest compositional gestures to the smallest details — from exposed, board-formed concrete walls and glass windows that disappear into nearly seamless corners, to the thatching on the exterior palapa, a freestanding Spanish open-air pavilion.

Interior floating walls stopping just short of the ceiling and the floating wood treads suspended in the steel stairway express the Modernist attention to detail. One such detail that might seem counterintuitive in a home that attempts to help transform a street into a neighborhood, reveals the complexity of the design. A sparkling sliver of glass, running the length of the roof before turning ninety degrees to dive down the front façade, splits the home's façade in two. Mediterranean influences dominate to the right, Modernist to the left, yet each side takes cues from the other. The metal grill on the left creates a cornice mirroring the wooden cornice on the right. To the left of the glass line, an exposed-wood box appears to float above the first story. Breaking down the volumes into smaller components acknowledges the neighbor on the left, a single-story residence. Across the street, two-story houses have begun to replace smaller homes, so this home's height also corresponds to this higher density. From the vantage point of its neighbors, the home asserts its own presence while making friendly gestures to its surroundings—the split that separates also binds, stitching the diverse neighborhood back together.

As the tall, split façade reflects the house's context, the palapa communicates the symbolically rich language of the heart — the analogue of the hearth. Even in this deeply symbolic center, the house draws on a mixture of Modern and Mediterranean vocabularies. The palapa references both California vernacular and Viennese avant-garde exemplified in Schindler's outdoor living room, replete with fireplaces and second story open-air "sleeping baskets." The thatched roof not only covers an exterior room; it roots itself in the ground and reaches into the trees. The floating box of the front façade allows second floor rooms to share space with the tree canopy and the inhabitants to engage nature in the tree life of squirrels and birds.

Nature is incorporated not only in the honest expression of materials, but also in the ways the home accommodates the elements: wind, sun, topography, and land movement. Sensitivity to the future of life on the planet and to nature were driving forces in the design. Sustainable materials, for the most part, available locally, are used throughout the home. The combination of concrete shear walls, steel framing, and wood framing can withstand the forces of high winds, three children, and a dog. Whenever possible and relevant to the design concept, materials are left exposed to reveal their natural finishes. Concrete floors with radiant heating smooth the transition from inside to outside while entire window walls open up to allow ocean breezes to cool the home.

Above all, this is a family home with a variety of experiences to choose from, ranging from cozy "cocoon" in the form of the palapa, to large, cathedral-like double height spaces. Asian antiques, Modern art, and family mementoes are an integral part of the material palette for a home designed to embrace the clutter of everyday life. Spaces are provided for artifacts and memories on the walls and horizontal surfaces.

The image of a tree house seems natural given the neighborhood's lush setting of mature palm, eucalyptus, and pine trees, and its panoramic position on a hill. Like a treetop hideaway, it provides views of both the ocean and the mountains, positioned to benefit from cooling ocean breezes and to resist fierce coastal storms. Exposed wood on the exterior of the floating box echoes the tree trunks, and, more subtly, the wood cornices are an abstraction of the forms of tree limbs.

The childhood dream of a tree house is a club you control the access to, but also share. This home with its tree house references is the neighborhood club that this family dreamt of — one that stitches together the diversity of the immediate neighborhood and the broader regional context. By encouraging neighbors, friends, and extended family to come and go, enjoy and share, it's where people want to be.

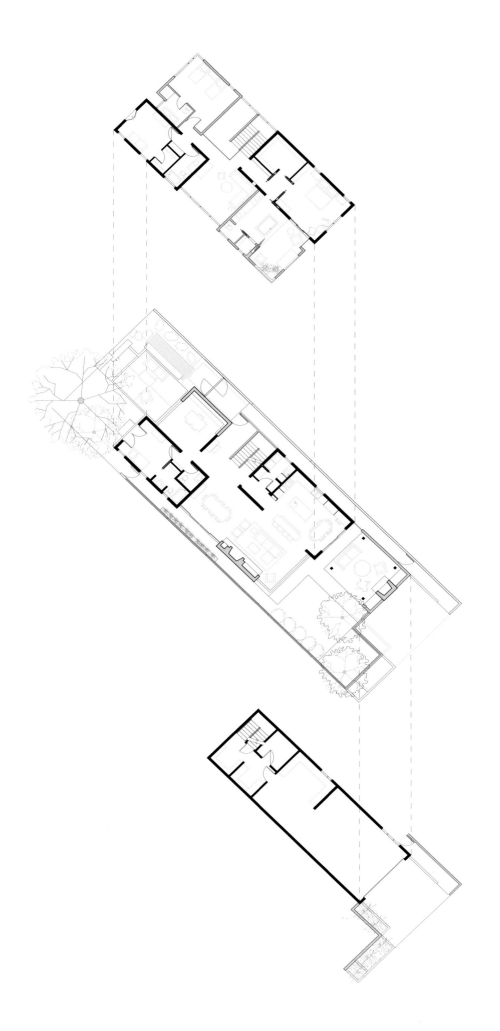

Whenever possible and
relevant to the design concept,
materials are left exposed
to reveal their natural finishes.
Concrete floors with radiant heating
smooth the transition from
inside to outside while
entire window walls open up
to allow ocean breezes
to cool the house.

What is the most ideal home for two professional athletes who, having dominated their respective sports, are at the top of their game and ready to start a family? What kind of setting would celebrate their strengths and achievements, rejuvenate them, and offer them a like-minded community and solitude simultaneously?

For their site they chose a location on the Strand — a pedestrian path extending several miles along the sand in the South Bay region of Los Angeles — where other residents share a desire for healthy living and actively engage in lively beach activities, outdoor parties in neighbor's front yards, rollerblading, jogging, volleyball, sunning, swimming, surfing, and sailing. The Strand is a highly dense, urban place to live; yet in the midst of all the action a home can also provide privacy and a safe haven from the outside world.

The lifestyle of the professional athlete is characterized by periods of intense physical exertion followed by periods of rest and nourishment of the body. Both facets of this lifestyle are supported by this home: the family has the option of spending time indoors or outside, in public or in varying degrees of privacy in the pool, spa, or ocean, and these choices are available year-round. In the middle of a neighborhood full of chaotic beach life, the home is a peaceful retreat where the environment encourages and facilitates healthy living.

To give the family breathing space, their home is sited on two contiguous parcels, breaking up the typical Strand configuration where homes often fill their lots with the maximum allowable square footage. On one of the two lots, the residence covers the allowable square footage with two floors of living space and a basement, while on the other lot the home retreats into a smaller volume adjacent to the court and pool, trading interior space to create the private courtyard and a single story living room. This organization provides a collateral urban benefit, a gift to the neighborhood by virtue of a public view corridor from city to sea.

Evoking these rarified and rustic lake districts associated with clean, pure water and clean, fresh air, the family named their oceanfront hideaway "Valhalla," the afterworld where Nordic heroes slain gloriously in battle dwelt.

The arrangement also defines a strong axial relationship between the city grid and the ocean horizon within the house itself. Both the front door and a second floor window seat located directly above it line up with a public stairway that climbs the hill directly behind the house. The window seat frames this stunning visual axis that stretches outside the house toward the volleyball nets next to the Strand, pushing the visual movement into the public realm of sports and sun and connecting the urban context with the Pacific Ocean. Directly in line with the volleyball nets, this spatial element aligns the home to other elements such as the piers that pull the eye out into the water, merging the urban with the natural, the cultivated with the wild.

This home revolves around a cool, clear pool, not unlike a glacial Scandinavian lake, with stone walls standing in for the steep alpine mountains that circle those deep water retreats. The pure geometry of the courtyard pool and spa walls creates a setting that seems to have been carved by forces of nature. The pool water laps directly against the rear retaining wall, and the intersecting spa is defined by lower stone walls, a striking union of earth and water that accentuates the glacial references. Evoking these rarified and rustic lake districts associated with clean, pure water and clean, fresh air, the family named their oceanfront hideaway "Valhalla," the afterworld where Nordic heroes slain gloriously in battle dwelt. A carved stone bearing this name is placed in the wall next to the street entrance. By choosing this designation, the family underscored the connections with the vision of rustic retreat and a healthy environment in the mountains with its more refined counterpart at the sea.

The main living space, designed with exposed wood beams similar to those found in a rustic cabin in the woods, surrounds the intimate courtyard enclosed by rough-hewn stone walls against which springs the deep blue swimming pool. A covered outdoor room, similar to a verandah built of heavy posts and beams, is adjacent to the main living space overlooking the pool and has an exterior fireplace. The covered patio softens the transition from outside to inside that extends from the quiet and contemplative enclosed yard to the living room and, eventually, to the active public areas of the Strand. This protected space affords the residents the option of retreating from the excitement while still enjoying the outdoors.

The combination of water, stone, and light elicit the physical and spiritual renewal made possible by the ceremony of immersing the body in water, outside, and surrounded by natural elements. Further enhancing the home's sense of well-being, the lower level beach room contains an elaborate spa, a temple to the body in a residence designed for a physically active family. The shower is devoid of doors, glass partitions separate the wet and dry spaces, and highly polished stone surfaces recall the rougher, exposed stone upstairs.

Throughout the house, understated finishes and materials complement strong wooden elements. The living room features high, beamed ceilings, a row of windows providing stunning uninterrupted views of the ocean, and a large fireplace surmounted by a cantilevered timber mantle that seems to have washed up on the shore. The oversized mantel emerged from the family's appreciation of a large wooden beam retained from the cottage that was previously on the site. The inclusion of this beam inspired a more rustic scale and rougher finishes throughout the house to contrast with the sleek modern appliances and the smooth stone floor. The stone wall in the living room forms a textured backdrop to the fireplace and its large wood mantel. The wall, in its material simplicity, stands as a sculptural element projecting outward into the courtyard linking the interior to the exterior. The entire design revolves around this free-standing plane, following in the tradition of Frank Lloyd Wright's Robie House, where the fulcrum for rotational movement is the central hearth. The powder room's sink, carved out of distressed wood, weathered and worn with time, refers back to the beamed ceilings and mantelpiece that reference a simple summer life in the high mountains of the Alps.

In their new beach home, this family is building on their professional success, bringing what they learned to this phase of their life. They can easily maintain the healthy lifestyle they have worked so hard to achieve and raise their family to share their appreciation for the benefits and wellbeing that result from pushing yourself to attain excellence in all areas of life.

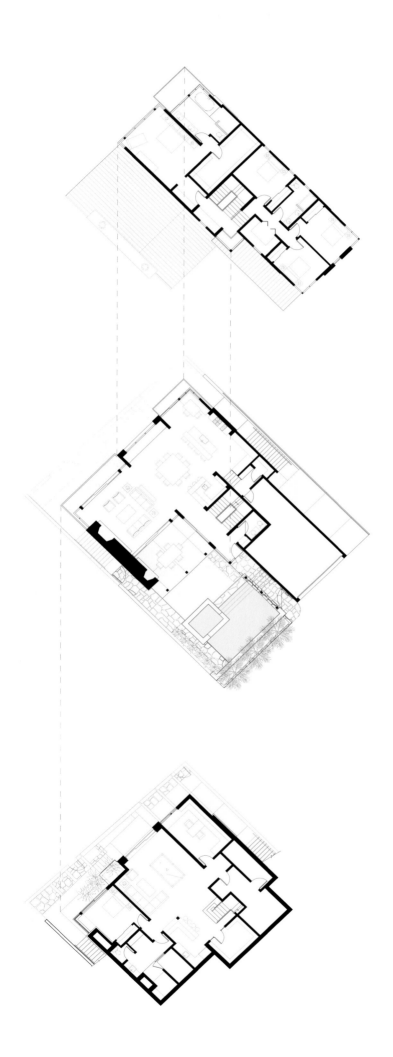

…a cool, clear pool, not unlike
a glacial Scandinavian lake,
with stone walls standing in for
the steep alpine mountains that
circle those deep water retreats.

From the time we are young children, we often imagine how our ideal, dream home would look. How would we live if we were free of any and all constraints and had to take only our own needs into consideration? What are the building blocks or elements that would create our vision of our own personal sanctuary? For those fortunate enough, fantasy can become reality, and reality can even surpass fantasy.

After raising a large family and leading a very active life together, this couple had the opportunity to construct a special place that would be primarily for themselves and not for the two generations of family who will come to visit. Having learned much from building several homes previously, they knew that they wanted something a bit smaller, but otherwise they were in a position to have whatever they wished, something tailor-made for the two of them in this exciting new phase of their lives.

Any dream home has to begin with the perfect setting. This property, overlooking the Pacific coast in Southern California, shares the same longitudinal coordinates and balmy Mediterranean climate with southern France. With breathtaking panoramic views sweeping from downtown Los Angeles to Palos Verdes Peninsula, Catalina Island, and the Santa Monica Bay, the home is like a belvedere — a place with a beautiful view or overlook.

The sounds of the fountains,
smells from the herb garden,
and the commanding view over the city
all awaken the senses to the possibilities
of an enriching, Provençal lifestyle
in Los Angeles.

Sited on a steeply inclined slope in the Santa Monica Mountains, this home evokes the image of a Paul Cézanne landscape painted in Provence. The sense of living in a French farmhouse or a Cézanne painting is so apparent in this house that it is almost as if it were taken directly from Peter Mayle's description of the Provençal house where he spent an enchanted year.

In this California interpretation of a Provençal house, a grand, elliptical staircase also rises up from a wine cellar, through a massive library of books set into the niches of a curved stone wall, weathered in hues of amber and gray. Attached to the lower level of this house, an enclosed courtyard borders a shimmering swimming pool fed by two fountains. Trellises and trees offer shade, while rosemary, tomatoes, and basil grow in the nearby kitchen garden, releasing an enticing aroma. The home basks in the sun in irresistible harmony with these gardens.

A stone base, in places up to two feet thick, supports the house, the solid portions of the building exterior underscoring the power and intensity of a south-facing exterior wall that opens up to the expansive views and brilliant light. The main living spaces are located on the upper level where the great room, formal dining room, kitchen, and breakfast room all look out above the lower-level rear gardens and survey the three-hundred-degree panorama through their shaded windows and covered balconies. The more private spaces reside on the ground floor behind the protective thickness of the stone base.

Placing the main living spaces on the entry level allows each of these rooms to be covered with a uniquely shaped ceiling that receives outward expression on the exterior silhouette as a cluster of roofs that have been progressively added to each other. Like the roofs of the Provençal farmhouse that grew from one small enclosure into a haphazard composition of many rooms, this house's roofscape indicates that the building grew over time into an irregular collection of volumes, reflecting the idea of collecting in its very form.

The rooms are extremely well-detailed, filled with special places — niches, vitrines, shelves, and alcoves — where the various artifacts the owners have gathered together across a lifetime are displayed. Majolica ceramics rest in an alcove near the kitchen, antique Chinese lunch boxes grace the breakfast parlor; and an antique Chinese horse terminates the long axis of the second floor. From antique oriental rugs to tapestry wall hangings, almost every surface of this house is layered in textile art.

The collections and interior furnishings are more than a mere accumulation of rare and beautiful objects. Rather, they bring together memories of travel, special occasions, and other lived experiences. The master bedroom features an antique dresser that was the first piece of furniture the owners bought in their married life. Sconces replicate a design found at the Flintridge Sacred Heart Academy in La Cañada-Flintridge, California, that one of the residents remembered from years past. A large armoire, acquired during a trip to Scotland, has become an integral part of the guest bedroom. Bathroom tiles, either antiques or based on antique patterns, lend a patina of collection and recollection.

This distinctive home, designed expressly for these two individuals, embodies their dream of the perfect residence for this stage of life. It reflects the gathering together of important memories, objects, and a community of friends and family into a residence that is also a sanctuary. The sounds of the fountains, smells from the herb garden, and the commanding view over the city all awaken the senses to the possibilities of an enriching, Provençal lifestyle in Los Angeles.

A stone base, in places up to
two feet thick, supports the house.
The solid portions of the building exterior
underscore the power and intensity of
a south-facing wall that opens up to
expansive views and brilliant light.

Close your eyes and consider for a moment how we navigate our cities. For example, in Los Angeles, it would not be inconceivable to hear someone say, "turn right at the giant doughnut" or "it's right next to the dentist's office with the giant penguin on top." Despite the availability of current mapping technology, it is more often the case that physical elements act as visual cues, making it easier for us to understand our environment, remember where we are, and focus on where we are going.

Like the legendary Lighthouse of Alexandria — strategically located on the coast — this successful entrepreneur's home stands sentry over the Santa Monica Bay and its immediate neighborhood, acting as a powerful symbolic element within its surroundings. More importantly, as his home base, it helps to keep him grounded and centered — a safe haven where he can escape his turbulent professional life, revitalize, refresh, and replenish body and soul.

At first a source of controversy among the neighbors, this home ultimately emerged as a refreshing new take on the local beach town context. A freestanding concrete wall shot up from the ground like a blade piercing the sky, appearing before any other part of this home's construction was complete. The wall loomed large, rough, and in stark contrast to the nearby wood houses. This was the first significant part of the home to be erected, and immediately the neighbors were furrowing their brows and rubbing their foreheads. The home's future resident also expressed concerns over the exposed concrete tower but after much discussion, everyone agreed to wait until the project was complete before initiating any drastic changes. Faith and patience were amply rewarded: more finished materials soon appeared in the home, yielding a sense of warmth: wide plank maple floors, solid block maple stair treads, a limestone fireplace, and a honed Brazilian granite fireplace. The raw, honest quality of the concrete took its place as a beautiful backdrop to these other, more refined surfaces.

Like the legendary Lighthouse of Alexandria, this home acts as a powerful symbol standing sentry over the bay and its immediate neighborhood.

The concrete wall centers and anchors the home, serving as its symbolic hearth. Upon entering, one encounters the fourteen-foot-wide, thirty-six-foot-tall, twelve-inch-thick slab that provides the background and support to an ascending stair. In a structural tour de force, a self-supporting steel plate bends twenty times to form a stair spanning from floor to floor, linking the entry to the upper living area. The combination of stair and wall forms a piece of freestanding sculpture, dramatically bathed in light and shadows from above. Where the slab's height impresses spatially, its slender depth impresses structurally, the architectural equivalent of an exposed spine. This is one of the house's defining moments, an object that transforms architecture into art.

Collaborating with one of the area's most accomplished builders working with poured-in-place concrete ensured that the home would be built with the utmost precision and close attention to detail. Such fine concrete craftsmanship places this residence within the larger architectural tradition of the Modern masters who have achieved elegant results with this material, from Louis Kahn to Le Corbusier to Tadao Ando. Here, as in the work of these preeminent designers, the concrete slab's industrial strength stands in powerful contrast to the finer grained finished material, emphasizing the tactile qualities of both.

Towers at the home's east and west ends contain, respectively, a balcony and a chimney that transform these symmetrically disposed volumes into asymmetrical façades. Exterior walls at the corners of the towers are pulled back to reveal their steel construction. They form a layered façade that recedes from the thick plaster surface to the metal frame and finally back to the glass pane. This deliberate erosion of the towers at the corners and windows offers a way, through construction details, to discover and comprehend the nature of the building's fabrication. By marking a prominent vertical plane, the towers reinforce the perception of the home as a landmark in the area.

The prominent front door and entry sequence, pitched roofs, and the chimneys evoke traditional images of dwelling, almost like a child's drawing of a house. In the dense lots of the Southern California beach towns, the living spaces often occupy the top floors to capture views of the horizon, surf, and sunsets. Here, the upper parts of the home create a distinct silhouette composed of pyramidal volumes floating above the public rooms. The teak-lined roofs on the corner towers are vaulted as clear spans without any horizontal members, creating sumptuous open spaces below.

In additional to its function as a personal refuge for its owner, the home is an impressive venue for entertaining. There are a variety of spaces to choose from, both indoors and out, each of which offer a unique experience. The upper terrace provides generous outdoor space, mirroring the remote access of an entry courtyard on the ground floor. A small balcony on the east tower and a terrace on the west façade permit the residents to communicate directly with the street below, as well as to survey the sweeping coastline and check out the local action. Because of the temperate climate in Southern California, these outdoor spaces are available for use in any season.

The completed home is a beacon of light standing tall in the neighborhood. It would not be a stretch of the imagination to conceive that, in the future, this contemporary, symbolic lighthouse will continue (to paraphrase Longfellow) to beam forth the sudden radiance of its light, with strange, unearthly splendor in the glare, long after its counterparts on the coastline have come and gone.

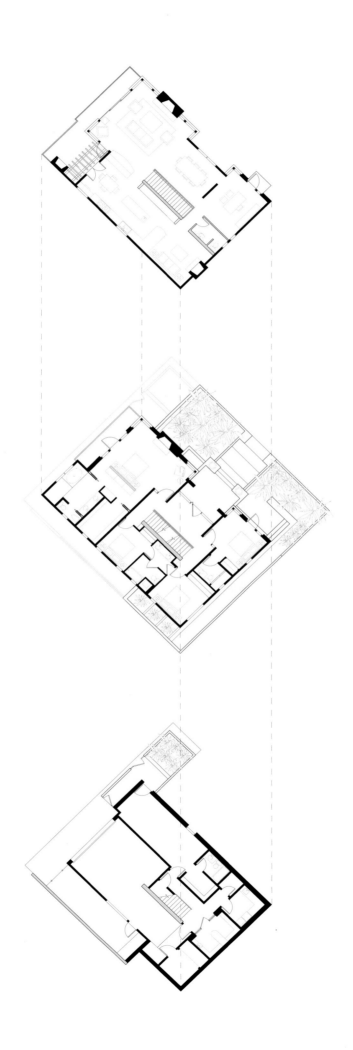

Where the slab's height impresses spatially,
its slender profile impresses structurally,
the architectural equivalent of an exposed spine.
This is one of the house's defining moments,
an object that transforms architecture into art.

Imagine what it would be like if you were a real-life rocket scientist, an aerospace engineer who is extremely bright, detail-oriented, and with an intense curiosity about a number of different subjects. Faced with the prospects of both an early retirement and the chance to build your dream home on the site of the bungalow you had lived in for several years, what would you do?

This particular rocket scientist seized the opportunity and threw himself into the project with all the excitement, passion, and quest for perfection with which he had once pursued his career. His approach to his home was similar to the way he would solve a scientific problem; diligently testing, working through, and solving different possibilities. This Southern California beach home, like the mind of its owner, is a study in rich contrasts, complex ideas, and meticulous details.

A number of oppositions — in styles of furniture, building materials, hard and soft edges, and levels of formality — add layers of surprise and intricacy to the home, expressing rigor, calibration, and a close attention to every aspect of design, while simultaneously reflecting comfort and relaxed beach living. Further contrasts occur between the efficiency of spaces tightly fitted with fine wood details and the expansiveness of larger, more rustic pieces that play off these delicate surfaces. The treads of the central stair are composed of large, raw, wooden blocks stacked on top of each other. In this highly crafted home, such elemental shapes become acutely expressive. The front door is a large rectangle divided into four sections by stainless steel inserts. Between the inserts, panels of wood grain are placed at forty-five degree angles to each other to emphasize the expressive potential of the material. In the living room, exposed wood beams hover above a single steel girder. This rigorous interplay between metal and wood, machined details and natural finishes, heightens the artistic characteristics of the design.

This Southern California beach home, like the mind of its owner, is a study in rich contrasts, complex ideas, and meticulous details.

Arguably, for most people the biggest attraction of living near the ocean is the extended view beyond their immediate world, seemingly into infinity. By opening up façades with large windows, extending interior spaces outward with balconies, and locating the more public spaces next to the beach, there are numerous opportunities to view the water. However, the design is intended not only to provide views of the ocean but also to be viewed from the beach. Plan and section interact within geometries of rectangles and squares as projected volumes of interlocking plaster and glass. Rooms that appear to be discrete entities in plan, step into each like three-dimensional puzzle pieces in section, forming intriguing sequences of adjoining rooms. Cantilevered balconies provide vantage points from which to survey the shore with L-shaped volumes of plaster and wood playing off these projecting volumes. The façade overlaps and interweaves into a formal composition that is as captivating to passersby as the interior is to the residents.

While the luxury of living on a site with an ocean view is the visual access to the water, at the same time the proximity to the sea necessitates protecting the home's interior and exterior from the damaging effects of the elements: sun, salt air, ocean spray, rainstorms, and blowing sand. The degree to which sunlight is allowed to enter the home is controlled with clever building articulation and planning as well as thermal glazing and shading devices. The building materials — hard woods, concrete, plaster, and glass — were selected, in part, to withstand these deleterious forces. Aluminum windows are covered with an electrically applied coating so the paint does not chip, and copper canopies similarly withstand the harsh coastal climate. Over the long term, these durable materials give back to the project economically and, ultimately, they contribute to the betterment of our planet by not having to be replaced or maintained on a continual basis.

The balance of highly designed rooms with opportunities for contingency and spontaneity is paralleled in the furniture choices. The sharp, crisp edges of two white leather Barcelona chairs (designed by Ludwig Mies van der Rohe in 1929 to serve as thrones for the King and Queen of Spain as the centerpiece of his famed German National Pavilion) and the soft edges of a comfortable green sofa echo the dialogue between purity and complexity, intention and improvisation, function and play that characterizes the entire home. The sofa sits on an exterior patio adjacent to a beach room that directly faces the Strand, opening up this highly ordered home to contingency, circumstance, serendipity, and chance. Containing a mid-century table, stone floors, cocktail bar, and a casual atmosphere conducive to relaxation, the room encourages the easy lifestyle of the Southern California beach communities. The Barcelona chairs are part of the furnishings of the more formal space of the living room.

Many seemingly disparate elements are assembled here under the same roof, yet the honest use of materials, precision of execution, and thoughtful interaction with the site produce a whole that is larger than the sum of its parts. The result of bringing together diverse materials, of marrying fine details and rustic materials, classic Modernist furniture and contemporary pieces, open casual spaces, and more formal rooms is a truly harmonious environment, one in which the inhabitants can grow and thrive. As the ancient Greek philosopher, Heraclitus, observed, the most beautiful harmony results from differences. When executed with great care and consideration, this is as true for architecture as it is for human relationships. This home successfully unites the rigor of an engineer's quest for exactitude with the architect's careful arrangement of inspirational forms — the perfect solution to the equation of a habitat for a former rocket scientist.

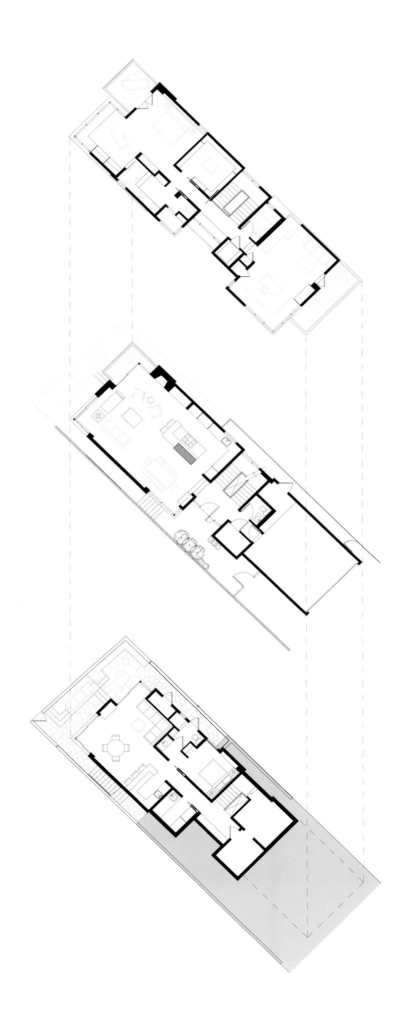

Rooms that appear to be
discrete entities in plan,
step into each other
like three dimensional
puzzle pieces in section,
forming intriguing sequences
of adjoining spaces.

Many seemingly
disparate elements
are assembled here
under the same roof.
The honest use of materials,
precise execution, and
thoughtful interaction
with the site produce
a whole that is larger
than the sum of its parts.

Breathtaking sites, an intentionally casual yet sophisticated elegance, an intimate relationship with nature, and a celebration of the temperate climate that allows a seamless fusion of indoor and outdoor living: these are hallmarks of what this region has to offer in terms of lifestyle. More than "houses," these homes are both personal sanctuaries for their residents as well as individual interpretations of the California Dream. They are the culmination of fruitful collaborations between our firm, KAA Design Group, and our clients who come to us with high expectations.

Much as the choice to reside in Southern California allows one to start life anew, collaborating with the design team to create a new home tailored specifically to one's needs offers the luxury of stepping back to consider and acknowledge priorities, goals, and the ways in which environments can both mirror and shape lives. It is a rare opportunity that neither we, nor our clients, take lightly. At KAA, we invite our clients to participate in the process of — what will undoubtedly be one of the most significant endeavors of their lives — the design of the environment in which they will feel secure, nurtured, and inspired so they can continue to pursue the new, the exciting, and the innovative. Our ultimate objective in designing homes, their interiors, and gardens is to expand and elevate the lives of our clients with whom we collaborate, and to facilitate their own process of self-discovery. This holistic approach yields unique solutions for each client, reflecting the individuality and range of their lifestyles.

Although our practice extends well beyond Southern California, it is rooted in and arises out of the expansive, continuously inventive, natural and cultural landscape of the area. The region's nurturing natural environment and open-minded atmosphere continues to foster a tradition of innovatively designed houses. With their experiments in residential design in the early- and mid-twentieth century, architects who worked in Southern California such as Rudolph Schindler, Richard Neutra, Wallace Neff, and George Washington Smith, continue to inspire research into new ways of living; one of the hallmarks of Southern California residential architecture. Like these trailblazers, we practice with an acute awareness of physical and historical context and a carefully considered use of local materials. Our work engages this rich tradition of innovation and experimentation, while responding to a climate of accelerated change. In each of our projects, we strive for a synthesis that is at once natural, sensitive, and creative; an accurate architectural expression of a way of life.

In this sunlit paradise of limitless possibilities, we feel fortunate to have so many opportunities to help others realize their dreams, often in ways they could never have anticipated.

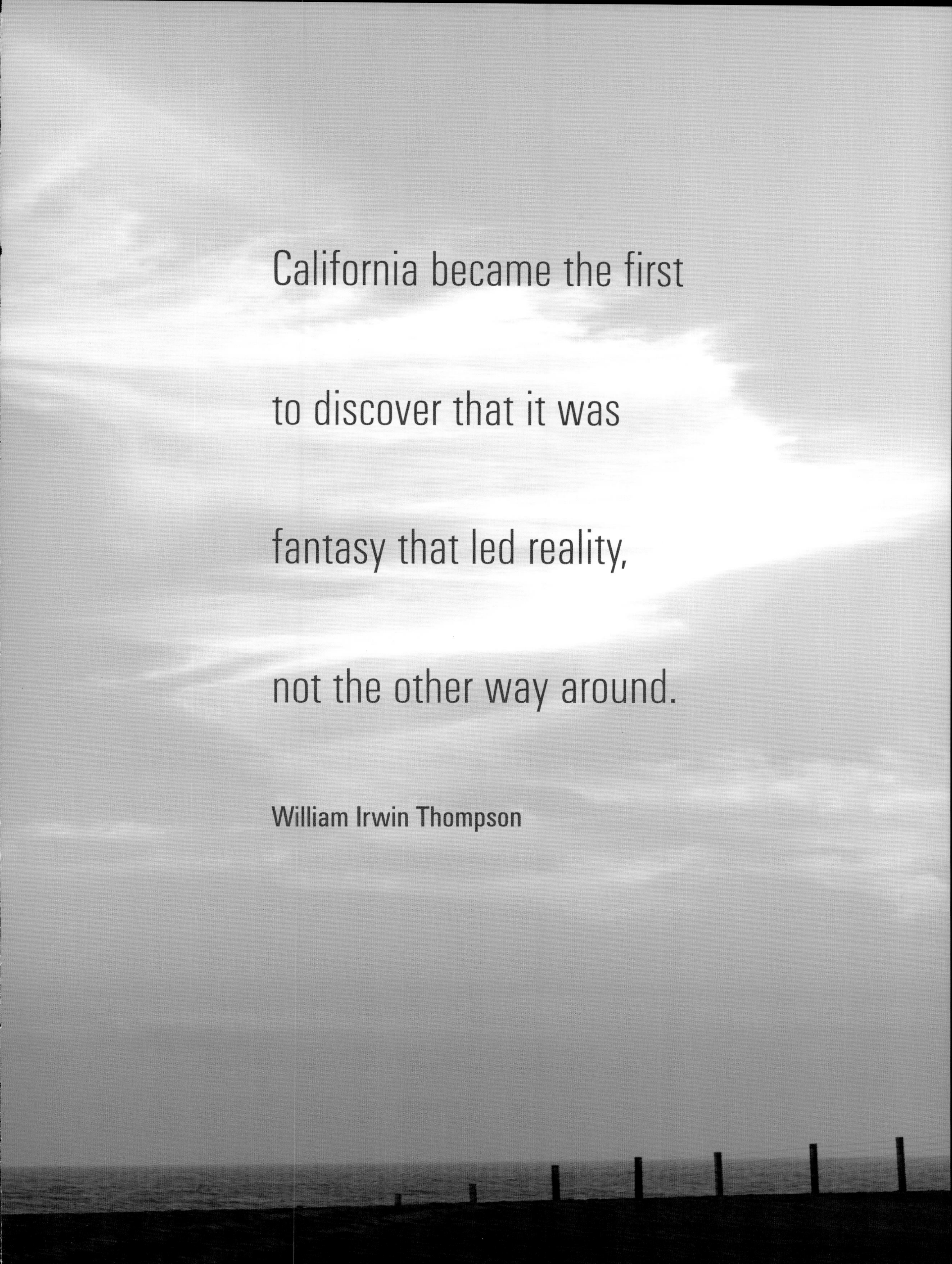

California became the first

to discover that it was

fantasy that led reality,

not the other way around.

William Irwin Thompson

Brian Adolph
Rogie Agustin
Diane Alexander
Barbara Alfors
Esther Alva
Carol Alvarez
Alex Anamos
Araceli Andrade
Meg Applequist
Eliseo Arebalos
Perla Arquieta
Patti Baker
Wesley Baker
Michael Ball
Chris Barrett
Philippe-Antoine Beauregard
Arin Binnarh
Sara Boruta
James Brencic
Vicki Byk
Sarah Calandro
Anne Carney
Louis-Philippe Carretta
Elayna Casey
Fernando Castro
Alexandra Cheng
Christina Cheng
Thomas Clapper
Beth Cofer
Jessica Comingore
Jennifer Conlon
Bradley Cooper
Elise Corvo
Mark Countryman
Martha dePlazaola
Michael Ellars
Kellie Eserts
Michael Eserts
Erik Evens
John Feldman
Shellie Fischtziur
Krista Flascha
Jeanne-Marie Fox
Robert Gdowski
Natalie Gearhart
Carlos Godinez
Kevin Goode
Jill Gordon
Debra Goto

Stacy Griffln
William Growdon
Nevert Guirgis
Russell Hatfleld
Lori Hays
Damon Hein
Mark Hembree
Que'Ron Hildreth
Alana Homesley
Daniel Hsu
Jennifer Hsu
Peggy Hsu
Duong Hua
Lisa Hunnicutt
Maria Iwanicki
Fred Jacksier-Chasen
John Jennings
Kelly Jimenez
Jennifer Johnson
Vince Jordan
Jennifer Kao
Judith Kim
Julie Lee Kim
Dara Kimball
Grant Kirkpatrick
Shaya Kirkpatrick
Hadi Koo
Angelique Kottke
Jenika Kurtz
William Laine
Shelly Lane
Erik Lang
Manolo Langis
Annette Lee
Lisa Lefevre
Braden LeMaster
Wendy Lumsden
Karen Madrid
Vaishali Makim
Vincent Manarite
Emily Maynard
Khaliah McDonald
Anthony McLin
Brandie Meis
Scott Min
Jessica Molina
Trisha Montesano
Luis Murillo
Alicia Nagel

Devanee Niednagel
Daryl Olesinski
Stephanie Osborne
Matthew Paola
Todd Paolillo
Amy Pawlowicz
Brian Pera
Anthony Poon
Suzanne Porush
Patti Poundstone
David Price
Jon Rahman
Christine Reins
Elizabeth Ricks
Jennifer Rimlinger
Michael Robbins
Melanie Robinson
Nazneen Sabavala
Miguel San Miguel
Naomi Sanders
Martin Schwanauer
Sharon Siegman
Deana Silverman
Kim Simerson
Voneelya Simmons
Art Simonian
Lily Sparks
Christopher Stage
Jonathan Starr
Stephen Straughan
May Sung
Duan Tran
David Vazquez
Alexander Vegh
Matthew Vincent
Kevin Vuong
Glenn Waggner
Kyle Wheeler
Benjamin Williams
Jerry Williams
Linda Wong
Steven Wunderlich
Issac Yates
Khin Zaw
Laura Zhao

It's all about the people. Twenty years of hard work and meaningful sanctuaries do not happen without an appreciation for collaboration, partnership, and diverse talent. At KAA, we think of our community of collaborators as both existing and evolving partners in our quest for design that elevates the human spirit. All are essential parts of the whole and, as we like to say, we are all in this together.

The essential KAAers who are or have been a part of our team through the years are listed on the preceding page. We would also like to thank our Principals and Associates Steve Straughan, Barbara Alfors, Luis Murillo, Patti Poundstone, Alex Anamos, Chris Barrett, and Melanie Robinson for their enormous talent and devotion.

Our Brand Experience Studio Director, Melanie Robinson, and her highly skilled team have infused their talent throughout this book and touch all points of our design work. Similarly, these and many other sanctuaries would be considerably diminished without the talent and spirit of our Landscape Studio, led by Damon Hein and Jerry Williams, and of our Interiors Studio, led by Chris Barrett.

Key to these projects and KAA's success is our close network of design and construction collaborators. All of these important team members have joined us on multiple endeavors herein, and we trust and value their contributions for these and our forthcoming sanctuaries:

For interior design, they include Tim Clarke of Tim Clarke, Inc., Mark Enos of Enos and Company, and Alana Homesley of Alana Homesley Interiors. For construction they include Dave Baldwin of Baldwin Construction, David Garinger of Garinger Construction, Peter McCoy of McCoy Construction, Rick Holtz of RHI Construction, Curtis Quillin of Quillin Construction, and Jeff Wilson of Wilson Construction. And we are deeply indebted to Dave McCarroll and his team at Kaplan, Gehring & McCarroll Lighting Design for gracefully bringing forth the light in these homes.

Several other collaborators have contributed to these personal sanctuaries including Swire Siegel Landscape Architects, Melinda Taylor Garden Design, Pacific Coast Landscape, and Susanne Devine of Devine Interiors.

This book celebrates twenty years of design by KAA, but key people have played a major role in helping to define the company in critical capacities beyond the design of our projects. They include:

Keith Granet, who has been an essential ingredient at KAA in so many capacities for so many years. It is simply not possible to list the gamut of his contributions.

Weldon Brewster, who has photographed our projects for two decades now. We have quite literally grown together in this design business, and it is a thrill to be featuring his photographic talent in the Invitation and Afterword portions of the book.

Our marketing team, Elizabeth Ricks and Brandie Meis, and their endless efforts and attention to detail.

Our writers, Deborah Fausch, Ph.D., and Paulette Singley, Ph.D., who contributed true insight into our work, and Linda Hart, Ph.D. who challenged us to get off the fence and speak from the heart.

Our book editor and producer, Brad Collins of Group C Inc., has been a patient and galvanizing force behind this book. We are grateful that we engaged his formidable voice and guidance.

Our Resourceress, Janet Sager of Sager/Monti, who guides and connects the specialized talent that seemingly knows no bounds in the design industry.

And to our key stakeholders and supporters, Bruce Meyer, Steven Spierer, Dr. Steven Sample, and Marc Appleton, for inspiration and mentorship.

And to all of our splendid clients who have entrusted us with the task of helping them pursue dreams, we feel fortunate to call you colleagues and friends.

Grant Kirkpatrick   Michael Eserts   Erik Evens
Founding Partner   *Partner*   *Partner*

Assassi © 08
Living Life on the Edge, all photos.
Valhalla, all photos.
Standing Sentry, p. 204, 207–213
Poetry in Precision, p. 214, 218–226, 230

© Weldon Brewster
Invitation image sequence, p. iv–xiii
Modern Legacy, p. 95
The Sentinel, p. 122 (left), 124, 126
A Gathering Place, p. 135
Belvedere, p. 182, 198
Standing Sentry, p. 200, 201, 206
Poetry in Precision, p. 215, 228, 232
Afterword image sequence, all photos.

© Jonn Coolidge
Cultivating Connections, p. 40
Poetry in Precision, p. 229, 231

© Grey Crawford
Belvedere, all photos except p. 182, 198

© Damon Hein
Cultivating Connections, p. 48

© Brandie Meis
Long title page, p. ii
Stirring the Melting Pot, p. 105
A Gathering Place, p. 129

© Erhard Pfeiffer
Interpreting a Dream, p. 54, 60–62, 64 (left), 70, 72 (left), 74
Modern Legacy, all photos except p. 95
Stirring the Melting Pot, all photos except p. 105
The Sentinel, p. 114–121, 122 (right)
A Gathering Place, p. 128, 132–134, 136–155

© Sharon Risedorph
Cultivating Connections, p. 22, 26, 27, 28 (right), 30–39, 40, 42–47

© Tim Street-Porter
Cultivating Connections, p. 18, 19, 24, 28 (left), 50 (left), 52

© Philip Clayton Thompson
Interpreting a Dream, p. 58, 64 (right), 66–69, 71, 72 (right), 76–78

© Dominique Vorillon
Cultivating Connections, p. 49, 50 (right)

Invitation

p. vii *Frank Lloyd Wright in Greg Bishop, Mike Marinacci, and
Joe Oesterle, *Weird California (Weird)* (New York: Sterling,
2006), 9. (Though not substantiated or corroborated
by the Taliesin Foundation, this quote is attributed to
Frank Lloyd Wright.)

p. ix Alison Lurie, *The Nowhere City* (New York: Owl Books, 1997).

Afterword

p. 237 Gerald W. Haslam, *Many Californias, Second Edition:
Literature From the Golden State* (Western Literature
Series) (Reno: University of Nevada Press, 1999), 171.

Published in Australia in 2009 by
The Images Publishing Group Pty Ltd
ABN 89 059 734 431
6 Bastow Place, Mulgrave, Victoria 3170, Australia
Tel: +61 3 9561 5544 Fax: +61 3 9561 4860
books@imagespublishing.com
www.imagespublishing.com

The Images Publishing Group Reference Number: 893

A Cataloguing-in-Publication entry for this title is available from the
National Library of Australia.

ISBN: 978 1 86470 368 9

Editing and production: Brad Collins and group c inc/New Haven, CT USA

Printed on 150 gsm Quatro Silk Matt paper by Everbest Printing Co. Ltd.,
in Hong Kong/China

IMAGES has included on its website a page for special notices in relation to this
and our other publications. Please visit www.imagespublishing.com.